Hunters
of the Sea

by Tony Bradman

illustrated by Giorgio Bacchin

CAMBRIDGE
UNIVERSITY PRESS

Institute of Education

One: Chill of Fear

My name is Sam Goodman, or at least that's what people call me these days. But I have had two other names in my life, and this is the strange tale of how I came by all three. You probably won't believe me, yet I swear that every word is true.

The first name I was called by is the easiest to talk about - it was the one given to me by my mother. I was born in Honolulu, the main town of the Hawaiian Isles. My mother was Hawaiian, and spoke the language of her people. So she called me *Ikaika*, which means 'strong'.

Sometimes I think she was wise to give me that name, because I needed to be strong from the start.
My father was an American sailor. He died when I was still a baby. His ship sank in a storm and he was drowned. That left us poor, and I grew up in the rough part of town, down by the harbour. We lived in a shack made from the driftwood that my mother collected on the beach, but she made it into a home.

The years went by, and we survived. My mother wove baskets to sell, and I did anything I could to help.

I went fishing, and I ran errands for the rich people in the town. The harbour was full of ships from all over the world, but I was always drawn to those from America - because of my father, I suppose. That's how I learned to speak the language of the Americans, a strange tongue they called 'English.'

Then one day, my mother fell ill with a coughing sickness. I wasn't worried to begin with - it had happened before but she had always got better. This time she didn't. She burned up with a terrible fever, and within a week she was dead.

At just ten years old, I was completely on my own - I was terrified. What would become of me? I had no idea what to do, so I sat by my mother's body for a day and a night. Eventually I realised I was hungry, so I went to find some food ...

That's when I found out people in this world, aside from my mother, of course, could be so very kind. Our neighbours helped me to bury my mother and happily gave me shelter, even though they had little room. Life went on, but Fate had something else in store for me.

One sunny morning, I went fishing, and then headed to the market to sell what I had caught. I was still on the road when three men stepped out from behind some palm trees and stood blocking my way. I could tell they were sailors from their clothes. At first I thought they might be lost, and simply wanted directions back to the harbour. But then I saw the grim looks on their faces, and I felt a sudden chill of fear.

'Well, what do you think, lads?' said one of the men. He was bald and hard-faced, and bigger than the others. He was clearly in charge. 'Will he do?'

'He's a bit scrawny, Amos,' said the second man. 'He might not last long.'

'We can't worry about that,' said the third. 'Old Coffin wants a boy.'

That name struck even more fear into my heart, and I started to back away.

'True enough,' said the one called Amos, shrugging. 'All right, lads - grab him!'

I turned to run, but it was too late. Strong hands seized me and a filthy sack was thrown over my head. Then, helpless to do anything, I was carried off.

Two: Kidnapped!

I was carried to a small boat and thrown into it. Even with a sack over my head I knew what a boat felt like, and I could smell the sea. The men rowed the boat out a short distance from the shore, and then the sack was pulled off.

I looked up, blinking in the sunlight, and saw the side of a ship looming high over me. 'Right, up you go,' said Amos. I shook my head and refused to budge. Amos sighed. 'It's either that or you'll be food for the fishes,' he said. 'I'm happy either way.'

So I did what I was told, and climbed the gangway. It was a big ship with three masts, and it had two longboats on its main deck. I realised instantly that it was a whaling ship - many such vessels called into the harbour at Honolulu. There were more men on the deck, most of them looking even tougher than the three who had seized me.

'What's this you've brought me, Amos?' said a loud voice. 'I told you to get a strong boy. This one is so thin, he'll probably get blown away in the breeze.'

I turned round. A tall man had come out of a doorway at the stern of the ship and was walking towards us. He wore a black coat with a high collar and shiny gold buttons, and he had a very hard, grim face. He stared at me with the coldest, meanest blue eyes I had ever seen.

'Sorry, Captain,' Amos said, nervously. 'He was the best we could find.'

'Really?' growled the Captain, glaring at him. 'Oh well, I suppose I'll just have to put up with him, then. Have you explained his duties to him? I hope he speaks English, anyway. I could barely understand the way last one talked.'

'I do speak English,' I said. 'Why have you brought me here? Why ...'

'SILENCE!' roared the Captain. 'You will only speak when you're spoken to, boy!

Raise the anchor, men. We have whales to catch and a fortune to make.'

The crew did as they were told. I heard the anchor
chains rattling, I saw the great white sails fill with
the wind, and I felt the ship begin to move. I had been
kidnapped, and there was nothing I could do about it.
Honolulu was soon far behind me ...

So began my days aboard the American whaling ship
Nimrod, commanded by Captain James Coffin
of Nantucket. At first, it was like a nightmare, and
I often prayed that I might wake up. I found out
the previous cabin boy had run off when the *Nimrod* had
docked in Honolulu, and I could see why. Captain Coffin
made me wait on him, morning, noon and night. He was
a hard taskmaster, and I never had a moment's peace.

It took me a while to get my sea-legs, too. I was
as sick as a dog for the first few days, and most
of the crew laughed at me. One man, called Sam,
was kind, though. He was older than the rest, and
was even brave enough to talk back to Captain Coffin,
sometimes. There were thirty-five men on board, half
from Nantucket, the rest from all over the world -
different parts of America, England, Spain, Portugal,
India, China, even other Pacific Islands. Nobody asked
me for my name. Somebody called me Shorty
one day, and soon everybody did the same, including
the Captain.

So that was the second of my three names, and before
long I got used to it. But I never, ever got used to what
happened when Captain Coffin hunted whales.

Three: A Wild Ride

As I say, I had seen plenty of whaling ships in Honolulu harbour. I had seen hundreds of barrels being unloaded from them, and I knew that those barrels contained whale meat and oil. But I had never thought about how the meat and oil got in them.

I soon found out. We found some whales a week after the *Nimrod* set sail from Honolulu with me aboard. The lookout in the crow's nest, high at the top of the ship's tallest mast, spotted them and called out, 'Ahoy down below! There she blows ...'

Everyone looked in the direction he was pointing. I was in the stern of the ship, standing behind Captain Coffin in case he needed me to fetch or carry for him. Amos was there too, holding on to the *Nimrod's* great wheel - that was his job as the ship's first mate. Captain Coffin raised his eyeglass and looked out over the sparkling waters of the Pacific. Then he lowered it again, and I saw he was grinning.

'Sperm whales off the port bow!' he hollered. 'Get us as close as you can, Amos!'

I went to the gunwale and looked out over the sea. I could hardly believe my eyes. Three enormous creatures swam in the blue sea just ahead of the *Nimrod*. They blew huge spouts of water from small holes in their heads, and smacked the water with their gigantic tails. As I watched, one slowly rolled on to its side and stared at me with a colossal eye that seemed to look deep into my soul.

I had never seen anything so amazing or so beautiful. And then, over the next few hours, I saw the exact opposite - something that utterly sickened me.

The longboats were launched and half a dozen men climbed down into each of them. Then the true chase began - the men rowing as fast as they could, Captain Coffin standing in the bow of one boat, holding a harpoon, and Amos doing the same in the other.

I had to look away when they threw their harpoons into the whales, the barbed blades digging into their flesh. The whales dived to try and shake them off, but each harpoon had a long rope tied to its end.

The whales dragged the longboats across the sea on
a wild ride. Eventually the whales slowed down,
seeming to give up and die.

Then came the worst part. The bodies were tied to the *Nimrod*, and we towed them to a nearby island. There, they were dragged on to the beach and the crew set to work cutting them up. Within a few hours, the men had filled a great number of barrels with meat and oil, leaving just the enormous skeletons of those beautiful creatures.

It was the saddest thing I had ever seen. I could feel tears rolling down my cheeks as my stomach churned with the awful stench. Sam explained that whales were worth lots of money, but only when they were dead. People liked eating whale meat, and they used the oil in lamps. In fact, almost every part of a whale was useful in one way or another. But hearing that didn't make me feel any better.

'Ah, so you don't like the way we make our living,' said Captain Coffin, scowling at me. 'Well, I can see I'm going to have to help you learn to love it.'

His words chilled me to the bone.

Four: A Kind Heart

From that day on, Captain Coffin made it his mission to toughen me up. He ordered me to take a place in his longboat crew, even though I could barely handle an oar. He didn't care about that, though. He only cared about how much money he was making.

Over the next few months we sailed all over
the wide Pacific, from the South to the North,
the West to the East. We chased every kind of whale
- Blue whales, Humpbacks, Right whales and Minkes
- and I soon learned to tell them apart. They were
different sizes and shapes. Some whales travelled in
big groups, others in just twos and threes, and they all
seemed to care for each other and their young.

I never learned to be like Captain Coffin. In fact,
the more whales I saw killed, the more I hated
the whole idea. How could anyone do such a thing?
But Captain Coffin just couldn't understand the way
I felt.

'What is wrong with you, boy?'
he growled. 'Men have always hunted
the creatures of the wild. We are
the hunters of the sea, the greatest hunters
of all.'

'There ain't nothing wrong with Shorty,
Captain,' said Sam, putting his arm round
my shoulders. 'You ain't going to change
him, either. He has a kind heart.'

'Well, a kind heart won't get you anywhere
in this world,' said Captain Coffin, glaring
at Sam and then at me. 'It's kill or be
killed, that's what I believe. You mark my
words, boy. The sooner you learn that,
the better off you'll be.'

Sam was right, though. I couldn't change,
and that just seemed to make Captain
Coffin even more angry. He terrorised
the ship, losing his temper at the slightest
thing and yelling at the crew all the time.
He even had a couple of the men flogged.

23

There was worse to come. A week went by without any sightings of whales ... then another week ... and another. The Captain's face grew more and more grim, and the men looked more worried than I had ever seen them before. The weather was hot too, the burning sun beating down on us day after day.

Then one day, the lookout in the crow's nest called out, 'There she blows - on our starboard!'

'They're Orcas, Captain,' said Sam. 'Why don't we just leave them be?'

I already knew Orcas didn't yield much meat or oil, so most whalers didn't go after them. But these were unlucky enough to have encountered Captain Coffin.

'Beggars can't be choosers,' he said. 'Better to have something in the hold that will make us some money, even if it's only pennies. Lower the longboats!'

When we got close, I saw there were five whales. One of them was small, just a baby, its mother trying to keep it close. I noticed she had a long white scar on her nose. Captain Coffin was standing with his harpoon raised, and aimed at the mother. She rolled on her side to look at us, and for a moment I felt as if our eyes met ...

I thought of my own poor mother and how she had tried to protect me. Suddenly I felt anger surge through me.

'NO!' I screamed, and grabbed the harpoon, wrestling it from the Captain's hands. He fell over backwards, but he was soon back on his feet and looming over me. I didn't care. The longboats had stopped, and the Orcas were making their escape.

But I knew there would be a price to pay, and that I'd be the one to pay it.

Five: Lost at Sea!

Captain Coffin was furious, of course. When we were back on the ship, he raged at me, and threatened me with all sorts of punishments. I expected to be flogged at the very least, but in the end he gave an order for me to be locked in a small cabin.

It was dark and dingy, and smelt strongly of tar and whale oil. I sat there alone for what seemed like hours, wondering what would become of me now. I could see no future for me on the *Nimrod*. Even if the Captain wanted to keep me as his cabin boy, I could no longer bear to be on his ship. But where in this world could I go?

After a while I realised the weather was changing. I could feel the ship beginning to roll - that meant the waves were getting bigger. Soon I heard the wind howling in the ship's rigging, and Captain Coffin yelling at the crew to take in the sails.

We had been in storms before, but never one like this.
Before long, it felt as if the ship was being picked
up by a giant and tossed from wave to wave. I was
thrown against the bulkhead several times, and started
to feel very frightened indeed. My stomach churned,
and I called desperately for someone to come and
release me.

Eventually, the door of the cabin was thrown open.
Sam stood there in front of me. 'Out you come, my lad!'
he said, shouting so I could hear him above the roaring
storm. 'You won't have a chance locked up in there if
the ship goes down!'

 I will never forget the sight that met me when I went
up on deck. The moon rode high in a dark sky and
the rain poured from ragged silvery clouds. Captain
Coffin stood at the wheel, fighting to keep the *Nimrod*
sailing on into the huge waves.

Then an even bigger wave hit us. The ship rolled over, and I was flung into the water. I went down, then bobbed to the surface just in time to see the *Nimrod* begin to sink, the waves pounding it into wreckage. At last, I managed to find a floating spar I could cling to - but I was lost at sea and sure that I would drown. I thought of my father, and how strange it was that I would die in exactly the same way as him.

I must have passed out, for the next thing I knew it was daylight. The sea was calm once more, and the sun beat down on me. Then I saw something that made my blood run cold ... the fin of a shark cutting through the water. Before long, there were more of them, perhaps a dozen, swimming around me. They came closer and closer, and I froze with fear, expecting to feel their teeth bite into me at any moment ...

Suddenly, a huge black and white shape burst out of the water and crashed down onto the sharks that were nearest to me. It was an Orca, and one I recognised, too. When she surfaced beside me, I saw that she had a white scar on her nose.

She wasn't alone. There were a dozen more like her, and though I know it sounds crazy, they fought to keep me safe. The sea boiled as the battle raged - Orcas crashing into sharks, the sharks snapping back at them. But the Orcas won in the end.

I found a piece of decking and climbed on. The mother Orca stayed to look after me. It seemed that the rest of the crew had gone down with the ship, and I shed some tears for Sam. I'm not sure how long I was in the water - perhaps a day and a night. And then, by some miracle, a ship appeared on the horizon. It was a trading ship out of New England, and the sailors hauled me aboard. The mother Orca followed the ship for a while - I watched her from the stern. Then another four Orcas joined her, including the little one. At last they flipped their tails, and were gone ...

There isn't much more of my story to tell. The trading ship brought me to America, where I stayed. I live on Cape Cod and I'm a fisherman. I called myself Sam, in memory of my friend on the *Nimrod*, and everyone says I'm a good man, so that's my third name - *Sam Goodman*. I have a wife now, and a son of my own, and I will make sure that he has a much better start in life than me. Sometimes I take him fishing with me, out on the ocean where the great humpbacks come to play and feed.

But the Orcas are still the most beautiful creatures I have ever seen.

PACIFIC OCEAN

ATLANTI

NEW ENGLAND

• NANTUCKET

HAWII

HONOLULU

W

E

S

38

39

Hunters of the Sea 🐟 *Tony Bradman*

Teaching notes written by Sue Bodman and Glen Franklin

Using this book

Content/theme/subject

This book follows the adventures of a young boy kidnapped and forced to work on a whaling ship. Written in five chapters, the story deals with sophisticated and complex themes, matched to the young reader's growing maturity.

Language structure

- Speech patterns and structures, such as *'You will only speak when you're spoken to, boy!'* (p.10) demonstrate character and motive.

- Sentences have greater complexity, with multiple clauses.

Book structure/visual features

- A strong plot and complex structure is supported by paragraphing and chapter organisation.

- Illustrations help to visualize the characters and settings whilst allowing for the reader's interpretation of events.

Vocabulary and comprehension

- Specific vocabulary choices serve to convey meaning and intent, as in the use of powerful verbs in reporting clauses, and to support the story setting and context: *'Ahoy down below! There she blows ...'* (p.14).

Curriculum links

Natural history – Whales are an endangered species. Use the story as a basis for investigations into conservation of the whale population. See, also 'Giants of the Ocean' (Gold Band) and 'Dolphins in the Wild' (Strand 3) in Cambridge Reading Adventures.

Learning outcomes

Children can:

- interpret indicators of character through dialogue and action

- consider the use of vocabulary and language structure to convey meaning

- view events from the perspective of each of the different characters.

Planning for guided reading

Lesson One: Characterisation through dialogue and action

Note – children will have read Chapter 1 (pp.2-7) prior to the first guided reading lesson.

Ask the group to review their reading of Chapter 1, and talk about their first impressions. Establish the period and setting: *What clues tell you that this story is set in the past? What have you learned about the boy already?* Talk about the idea that he has three names, and predict how that might be possible.

Turn to p.6. Consider how the characters are portrayed, through their speech (*'All right lads – grab him!'*) and their actions. Look also at how the illustration supports the description in the text.

Turn to p.8 and ensure all children understand what a whaling ship is.

Set an independent reading task to read Chapter 2. Ask the children to pay particular attention to how Captain Coffin is introduced on p.10.

Bring the group together and clarify anything the children found problematic when reading. Review p.10 together, looking at the description of Captain Coffin. Turn to p.13 and discuss how the boy got his second name. Have the children summarise the story so far.

Follow up after the lesson: Children reread Chapter 2 and pre-read Chapter 3. Prompt them to note particularly effective language